THE
NEW RIGHT
image and reality

Gerald Cohen
Nicholas Bosanquet
Alan Ryan
Bhikhu Parekh
William Keegan
Franz Gress
with an introduction by Nicholas Deakin

Contents

Note: The views expressed in this publication are those of the authors and not necessarily of the Runnymede Trust.

Published by The Runnymede Trust,
178 North Gower Street, London NW1 2NB.

May 1986.

ISBN 0 902397 61 3

Cover designed by Susan Hobbs.

Typeset and printed by The Russell Press Ltd., Nottingham.

Introduction

There is a widespread view now abroad that in the debate about the future of British society the New Right has seized the intellectual initiative. On closer inspection, this view turns out to owe a good deal to self-sustaining publicity, notably that of the Institute of Economic Affairs, maintained in circulation by credulous journalists and the efforts of those individual New Right polemicists who enjoy ready access to the national press. However on one question there is little room for doubt; the ideas being advanced by the New Right have achieved wide circulation and have been influential at least in the minimum sense of being widely discussed and repeated — if sometimes uncritically and without a full appreciation of the complicated issues that lie behind them. At the same time there has been a shortage of exciting new ideas emerging from the more traditional liberal or left positions, either in this country or in Western Europe. The same is also true, though to a lesser degree of the United States. To this extent at least, the claim recently made by the Prime Minister to have created a 'new consensus' may have some foundation.

The time is accordingly ripe for a re-examination of the ideas being advanced by the New Right that is not based merely on gossip about the personalities involved and does not treat the process by which the New Right has obtained its influence as some conspiracy laid down in hidden Protocols of the Elders of Lord North Street. In that belief the Runnymede Trust (which is an independent charitable body) recently brought together a group of people whose recent or current work has been undertaken in areas which have been the subject of concern to the New Right. Six papers were presented to a seminar organised by the Runnymede Trust at All Souls College, Oxford in July 1985 and attended by a wider gathering of specialists; an edited version of those papers, together with some of the contributions made in the course of discussion, form the substance of this pamphlet. The Trust believes that, taken together, these papers make a significant contribution to a debate of considerable intellectual and practical importance.

Two of the papers, those by GA Cohen and Alan Ryan, address the issues that emerge on the philosophical higher ground, an area where the

New Right has been especially active. These papers are complemented by two contributions exploring the applications of New Right theories in particular policy areas — economic policy (Nicholas Bosanquet) and race relations (Bhikhu Parekh). Finally William Keegan explores the relevance of New Right views to the current political scene and Franz Gress draws some comparisons with similar developments in Europe. A further comparison that might well have been made is with the situation in the United States; and some contributors do make reference to that; but the links have been thoroughly explored elsewhere, most recently by David Edgar in his valuable contribution in 'The Future of the Left', which having earned the accolade of being described as tendentious by the Salisbury Review, the main intellectual organ of the New Right, may reasonably be assumed to be authoritative. It was therefore not felt necessary to go over this ground again.

The comparative perspective is of particular value in providing a reminder that we in Britain have been spared the sharpness of the choices that faced our European opposite numbers fifty years ago, when decisions about issues in political philosophy could literally become matters of life or death. The corollary is that the right in Europe has taken forty years to shake off the stigma of collaboration with fascism and Nazism. That issue does not arise, or at least not in the same extreme form, for the right in Britain, where the last relics of prewar fascism, as incarnated in the British Union of Fascists, disappeared when Oswald Mosley was detained under regulation 18B in 1940. Hence, whatever the position in Continental Europe, fascism in its 'classical' anti-semitic form is not one of the strands that goes to make the position of the contemporary New Right in this country, which has kept conspicuously clear of the attacks on Jews that have marked some of its European equivalents. Yet Vichy's 'Travail, Famille, Patrie' would in many ways be an appropriate slogan for the British New Right. And anti-immigrant sentiment, directed at the postwar immigration from the New Commonwealth, is of course quite another matter as Bhikhu Parekh clearly demonstrates.

In spite of the absence of some themes that are present in other right wing groupings elsewhere, the diversity of perspectives to be found in the British New Right is quite sufficient to make it difficult to produce a clear cut definition of the New Right's philosophy and general approach to political and social policy questions. On this, as on several issues, the contributors to the Seminar were divided: some, like Alan Ryan, feeling that concise summary of the New Right position could be achieved; others, like Bhikhu Parekh, that the range of views is too great to make the attempt worthwhile. But, having said this, most of the contributors were prepared to recognise three distinct strands of opinion which, if drawn together, make up a position which could be identified with the

New Right: a laisser-faire economic strand; a moralistic position on social policy and a strong commitment to nationalism and the authority of the Nation State.

Such a definition has the interesting consequence of bringing together those who explicitly define their position as 'Conservative', like Roger Scruton, and those who emphatically refuse that description, like Hayek. But it also excludes some of the libertarians, like Nozick, or the extreme version of the same tendency in Europe described by Franz Gress — the 'Gramscistes de droit'. For one of the touchstones for inclusion is a belief in the role of the State and the key distinguishing factor the functions that are assigned to it.

This in turn is where some of the inconsistencies within the body of views identified with the New Right emerge. In a recent article in the New Right's theoretical journal, David J Levy writes that: 'under the influence of the generally sound economic doctrines associated with the name of Hayek, Friedman and the IEA, conservatives in recent years have allowed their political rhetoric and, therefore, popular perception of their practice to become dominated by an unhealthily negative view of the State'.

At the same time, economic policy, as reflected in the present Government's practices, has begun to lose some of its original commitment to economic liberalism in its pure, Chicagoan form and become more pragmatic, at least in presentation (the abandonment of M3 as a measure of the money supply and hence as an instrument of policy being the most obvious recent example). Hence we have it, on Roger Scruton's authority, that the Government now displays 'the traditional pragmatism of the Conservative Party and its ideology is no more than an expedient'. This may in some ways be just as well, since the gap between pure economic liberalism and the increasingly strong commitment of the Government and its supporters to state intervention on a constantly growing list of issues of public and private morality has been growing steadily wider. This was recently neatly summed up by an editorial in the *Times* which proclaimed ex cathedra, apropos of admission charges to museums, that 'people are the better for paying for their own needs and pleasures'. The application of this principle to the area of sexual behaviour would produce consequences unlikely to commend themselves to those members of the Government who are anxious, in David Edgar's felicitous phrase, to see the state move 'out of the boardroom and into the bedroom'. However even such evident inconsistencies are unlikely to spare us the ridiculous spectacle of Norman Tebbit in a fit of morality, trying to keep his balance on both circus horses at once.

This leaves the third area of strongly held beliefs, which centre round the concept of nationhood. As Michael Ivens, the economic propagandist, recently observed in the *Salisbury Review*, 'what Conservatives should conserve is not the outer form of institutions but their inner spirit, and the underlying sense of unity between the individual and the tribe'. This, I suspect, is likely to stand as the New Right's most significant achievement — it is difficult to deny that the last decade has seen a strong revival of nationalism and traditional patriotic sentiment. The key question here is who has profited from this growth, apart from some 1400 sheep farmers in the South Atlantic. Certainly, it is very clear who has not gained. As Bhikhu Parekh demonstrates, the new nationalism is excluding, not incorporating, and deeply sceptical of the claims of those with the 'wrong' skin pigmentation to belong to the 'tribe' (to adopt Ivens' term).

It is in the hope of providing further clarification on these, and many other issues that the present collection is now offered. In particular, given the currency that the ideas put forward by the New Right have secured both among influential people and in the press it is important to show what the consequences of these ideas are in particular policy areas, as Bhikhu Parekh has done in this collection for the field of race relations. As he demonstrates these consequences can be both direct and indirect, in that the intellectual tone and associations of this set of ideas can encourage the expression of hostility and the promotion of authoritarian policies towards minorities of all kinds.

How far the rise of the New Right and the policies associated (often rather loosely) with it is a temporary phenomenon or how far it represents a permanent change in the structures and values of our society — a paradigm shift, in the recently fashionable phrase — is still a matter for debate. Hence the value of William Keegan's contribution to this collection in which he shows how the influence of New Right ideas has ebbed and flowed during the present Government's period of office. But what is important is that broader debates should now be taking place, and on the basis of coherently argued positions. If their challenge to established modes of thought — liberal, radical, socialist and indeed conservative — helps precipitate such debates, and in turn produce a new range of positive ideas about the future aims of society, the New Right and its supporters can fairly claim to have rendered the State — though perhaps not the kind of State they have in mind — some service.

Nicholas Deakin

The Ideas of Robert Nozick
Gerald Cohen

The work of the American philosopher, Robert Nozick of Harvard University, has had great influence not only in the United States but among moral philosophers, political thinkers and some practising politicians in the United Kingdom. The general thesis of his book *Anarchy, State and Utopia* is a justification of inequality in society. Gerald Cohen, Professor of Social and Political Theory at Oxford University, examines Nozick's views on personal freedom and property.

One way of doing philosophy well is to assemble premises which even opponents will not want to deny, and, by dint of skill at inference, to derive results which opponents will want to deny but which, having granted the premises, they will be hard pressed to deny. In mildly technical jargon, the trick is to go from weak premises to strong conclusions. It is no trick at all, of course, to go from premises which are already controversial to strong conclusions.

Now some critics of the influential Harvard new right philosopher Robert Nozick dismiss his work as belonging to the second category just distinguished. Thomas Nagel for example, avers in his review of *Anarchy, State and Utopia*, which appeared in 1974, that Nozick's strongly inegalitarian conclusions are boringly unsurprising in light of the strongly inegalitarian premises with which he begins. But I believe that Nozick can be presented more sympathetically than that, and that he needs to be so presented in order that we may understand the otherwise unaccountable power of his ideas. Speaking personally, I was raised in a Marxist home and I was bored by academic political philosophy until I read Nozick, who roused me from my dogmatic socialist slumber. For ten years I have been engaged in battle against his ideas, and I have, I think, made some progress. What I should like to do now is to lay out those ideas as persuasively as I can, reserving most of my criticism of them for the discussion, if critical interventions from me in the discussion prove to be appropriate or necessary.

Speaking rather broadly, Nozick's aim is to defend the inequality which makes socialists angry and liberals uneasy by exploiting the

9

commitment to freedom which is common to socialists, liberals, and rightists of the Nozick free-market-supporting kind. There exist other kinds of rightists, such as Scruton, who effect scepticism about freedom itself, but, whatever impact they have achieved on contemporary upper middle-brow intellectual culture, they do not, like Nozick, disturb socialists and liberals intellectually, precisely because they do not pretend to build their edifice on shared normative foundations.

But how does Nozick go from freedom to inequality? He departs from essentially two premisses, the first of which is that no one should be a slave, in whole or in part, to anyone else. No one, that is, may rightfully be owned by anyone else, but each is, rightfully, a self-owner. This means that each may treat his own person and powers as he may treat anything else of which he is the legitimate owner. Suppose I am the legitimate owner of a knife. Then I may do what I like with it, provided that I do not harm anyone else with it; and so, in particular, I may not be required to put it at the disposal of anyone else, or to use it on behalf of anyone else, on pain of coercive penalty, unless I have contracted to do so. If I own a knife, and you, who have no knife, desperately need to cut something, then it might be unpleasant or even immoral of me to withhold the knife from you, but, I being the knife's owner, you may not force me to lend it to you, or you may not get other people, such as the State to apply force to me on your behalf. So, similarly, if I am not a slave, but a sovereign self-owner, then you may not co-opt my services when I have not contracted to supply them. If you had the right to command them independent of contract, then I would be, to that extent, your slave. It supposedly follows that a welfare state, in which, for example, quadriplegics are sustained by income extracted from the able-bodied on pain of coercive sanction, involves the partial slavery of some to others. It involves, so the Nozickian would contend, exactly that subordination of some to others to which socialists object when they plead against the power of capitalists over workers. Yet that is a legitimate power, being the fruit of contract, whereas no contract is involved as background to the service which the welfare state demands.

We may summarize this first part of Nozick's argument as follows:
 (1) No one is to any degree the slave of anyone else, therefore:
 (2) No one is owned, in whole or in part, by anyone else, therefore:
 (3) Each person is owned by himself, therefore:
 (4) Each person must be free to do as he pleases, provided only that he does not harm anyone else: he is not required to help anyone else.

I come now to Nozick's second premiss. Whereas the first premiss is about people and their powers, the second premiss is about everything else and its powers, which is to say that it is about nature and about the unmodified resources of nature. These, for Nozick, are antecedent to anyone's actions or labour on them, not owned by anyone. They preexisted the appearance of human beings in the world, and while each human being is born with the natural rights over himself implied by the first premiss, none is born with any natural rights over things. Hence each is entitled to appropriate any amount of raw material resources, provided that, since (4), which is a consequence of (1), must be respected, he does not thereby harm anyone, including within 'anyone' not only those who are around when the appropriation occurs, but also anyone who comes later. So the second premiss is:

> (5) The external world, in its native state, is not owned, in whole or in part, by anyone.

And (5), together with (4) enables inference of

> (6) Each person may gather to himself unlimited quantities of natural resources provided that he does not thereby harm anyone.

The next step requires a view about what it means to harm somebody by appropriating an unowned natural resource. Nozick's answer is that it is to make him worse off than he would have been had the resource not been appropriated. But unappropriated resources, like common land, tend to be used less productively, for incentive reasons, than resources taken into secure private control and therefore transformable for private gain. It is relatively easy to secure so much gain from their private exploitation that their private appropriators will have enough to compensate non-appropriators for their loss of free access to resources. Non-appropriators will then not be worse off than they would have been had the resources not been privately appropriated. A commonly owned beach will suffer from litter and other disamenity, since no one will have an incentive not to litter, it being more costly for him to avoid littering than to suffer the miniscule extra disamenity his own litter produces. A private appropriator can see to the litter and charge for access to the beach at a price at which he gains and nobody on balance loses since a litterless beach is worth something to everybody. Thereby he establishes private property in what no one owns without harming anyone. And the argument easily generalizes to justify the comprehensive privatization of everything, by those who are quick enough to privatize before others do. Some, who form what we may call a proletariat, will have been too slow or will have been born too late to privatize anthing, but they will not be relevantly worse off, so they have have no just grievance to press. In sum, (6) enables inference of

> (7) Unequal quantities of natural resources may, quite readily and legitimately, become privately owned by a section of the population.

Now if each owns himself, in the sense of (4), and the resources of the external world are monopolized by a section of the population, the resulting economy will, on ordinary assumptions about human motivation (which is to say, on the assumption that people are not extraordinarily altruistic), exhibit extensive inequality of condition, on any view of what equality of condition is, be it equality of income, or of utility, or of need satisfaction or whatever. So (4) and (7) yield the conclusion, which is that:

  (8) Extensive inequality of condition is unavoidable, or avoidable only on pain of violating people's rights to themselves and to things.

Now, in my own academic work I have been concerned to defeat Nozick's line of argumentation. I think we can resist it in at least three ways. The first is to challenge the derivation of (4) from (1), and, more generally, to challenge the rhetoric of self-ownership. But I think it is interesting and important that we can resist Nozick in two decisive ways which involve no rejection of the self-ownership idea. One is to challenge his notion of harm, by means of which he passes from (6) to (7). One can question the test Nozick uses for determining whether an appropriation of private property harms someone, and argue, against him, that the fact that a person is no worse off than he would have been had the resource not been privately appropriated is an insufficient demonstration that he is not harmed.[1] And the other way of objecting to Nozick without questioning the idea of self-ownership is to challenge his second premiss, (5), the premiss that the external world is originally unowned. Of course, it is, legally speaking originally unowned, but we are not here discussing its original legal condition, but rather its original moral condition. If we were discussing legal, as opposed to moral, truth, then the claim that people own themselves would also be false. One may, then, press against Nozick an alternative view of the original moral relationship between people and things, under which we regard nature as, from the start, collectively owned by everyone. If that different conception of rights over the world is united with the principle of self-ownership, extensive inequality of condition is avoidable.[2]

1. This objection is elaborated in my 'Nozick on Appropriation', *New Left Review* No. 150 March/April, 1985, pp.89-107.
2. For a development of the argument for that conclusion see my 'Self-Ownership, World Ownership and Equality', *Social Philosophy and Policy,* 1986.

Answers to questions

Q. To what extent, according to Nozick, are the state's activities legitimate?

A. The activity of protecting private property is legitimate, and the activity of protecting people from aggression threatened by other people is also legitimate. The State has, moreover, the legitimate task of rectifying past injustices. Thus Nozick, as a theoretician, is prepared to recognise that the past history of the United States has involved a great deal of injustice and dispossession and consequent unacceptable disadvantage which his principles would not justify, but condemn. He says at one point in his book, *Anarchy, State and Utopia,* that the welfare state, which can't be justified on the sort of grounds on which socialists and left-wing liberals would seek to justify it, could be justified as a temporary measure, to rectify past injustices. But though that's a part of his theoretical position, the practical impact of the theory is different, and his own political allegiance belies it. Nozick joined a small political party in the United States called the Libertarian Party whose policy would be to dismantle the welfare state, a policy which his theory, because of its recognition of past injustices, doesn't justify. In this country, too, there are quite a lot of libertarians whose official theory is consistent with quite radical action of a remedial kind by the State but if you argue with them about any particular current policy issue, they tend to take a line which ignores that official commitment. That is, at any rate, my own experience.

Q. Does anyone have to pay for the protection the State is supposed to offer? And what about defence policy? And the State's right to restrict immigration?

A. Of course, you have to pay for the protection the State gives to your person even though you don't have any private property. I can't remember whether there is a discussion in Nozick of the appropriate rates of tax, of whether, for example, people who have more property protected have to pay higher tax.

The various sorts of semi-lunatic, libertarian, American publications that one looks at from time to time do take an extraordinarily radical line both on defence and on immigration. They say that the State has no right to set itself up in contention with other States independent of the voluntary subscription of individuals that it should do so, so defence goes by the board. They also say that nobody has the right to restrict the freedom of movement of people from one place to another. So you get an extraordinary conjunction of views, which might have a consistent rationale running through it, but which is politically peculiar.

Q. What would Nozick say to a new social contract, unanimously entered into by a population to instal a welfare state?

A. He would say that it is utterly and entirely legitimate. And he would also correctly predict that it is not going to happen.

13

Q. The notion of belonging to other people in the sense of belonging to a family or community, seems to be missing from Nozick's thesis.

A. I don't agree that Nozick's individualism negates community and communal values. Let's take your own illustration: belonging to a family. I belong to my family and that means I feel special obligations towards its members. But it doesn't mean that I think it would be appropriate for me to be forced to carry out all those obligations. I have duties of care towards my children the non-performance of which should not result in fines and imprisonment and so forth. Again, if I make a promise to somebody, then there is an important tie between us, but it doesn't follow that if I break the promise then I should suffer a legal penalty. Nozick would say that his individualism is consistent with community. He would say: I'm not against community. If people like community they are welcome to enjoy it with one another. You have to argue for something stronger, which I think *could* be argued for, namely a community whose coherence is in certain respects enforced. Nozick would say: look, if it is a genuine community, it can't be a community by virtue of enforcement. If the people really feel united with one another why does their unity have to be enforced? If they feel united, then a welfare state is unnecessary because there will be voluntary charity to care for the disadvantaged. You cannot say that all your obligations are ones that it would be legitimate to enforce. So what you have to show is that it is appropriate to enforce communal obligations, in face of the challenge that their enforcement might be thought to detract from their communal character.

Q. You say the attraction of the Nozick position is that it picks up something we believe. But I don't know anybody who thinks we own ourselves.

A. No, I don't myself believe it. But I do think many people find it attractive or plausible, and not just philosophers, but ordinary people. They may not use the language of ownership, but that language is quite dispensable. What many people believe is that I alone have the right to decide what should happen to my own person and powers.

Q. Nozick seems to select his own standard quite arbitrarily for deciding when people are better off or worse off. In the example you have of the beach, a poor family might want to bathe on a litter-strewn beach so long as they could bathe without paying for it.

A. Well that particular family has to be let in free on Nozick's principle. But his argument is that most people won't be like them. Still, I think there's a big cheat going on in his move from (6) to (7): Nozick's criteria for harm are too narrow. For he only compares what things are like after a certain person has appropriated the resource with what they would have been like had nobody appropriated it. And that leaves out of account the possibility that somebody else might have appropriated it. Why should I not consider, in estimating whether I have been harmed, what might have happened had I got there first, and what might have happened had we collectively appropriated it because we felt it wasn't right to have a principle of 'First come, first served'? So I think that is one way to attack Nozick without denying the claims about self-ownership. It also doesn't require asserting that people have rights in external things antecedent to anyone's action on them.

Q. But you said earlier that the language of ownership was dispensable.

A. I have to modify what I said. I think the move from (2) to (3) probably requires the false idea that it is appropriate to talk about ownership here, because only when you have that idea can you go from 'Well, nobody else owns me' to 'Therefore I own myself'. One might say instead that nobody owns anybody. But I still think that the essence of the case can be put forward in terms of certain claims about people's rights, without mentioning ownership. You can start with (4) and treat (4) as a statement of what people's basic rights are and I think you could recruit a lot of agreement to (4). A lot of people think that the only enforcible obligation human beings fall under is they mustn't harm other people. And that seems to me to be the conceptually essential claim.

Q. Nozick's argument seems completely unhistorical. Man in the Greek conception was always part of society and the State. In a modern State, his model of self-regulation is simply not possible. The contract theory was always a fiction.

A. Well you raise questions there about the whole status of Anglo-American analytical political philosophy. Nozick's work is not distinguished in the respect you emphasize from the works of Rawls or Dworkin or other major non-right-wing contributors to Anglo-American political philosophy. You raise such a vast question that all I can say is that, unlike many people who are inclined to support socialism, I would not myself make the sort of critique you make. Methodologically, we are at odds. But I realise that this is a huge issue, and that I've done nothing to settle it here.

Hayek and Friedman
Nicholas Bosanquet

The economic and social theories of Friedrich Hayek and Milton Friedman have had great political influence over the last decade in many countries particularly in the United Kingdom and the United States. They have affected attitudes and policies towards racial minorities, often indirectly but in important ways. Nicholas Bosanquet, of the Centre for Health Economics at York University, considers their views.

I want to ask if Hayek and Friedman have anything relevant to say about the problems of racial equality and race relations in Britain and the United States. I shall deal quite quickly with Hayek, because although by inference and by implication there are some interesting conclusions for race relations in Hayek's thought there is nothing directly there, while in Friedman there is a great deal of specific writing on the problems of race relations in the US. To give him credit this goes well back before the subject became popular or a central one in American politics.

Hayek's thought really started from a critique of socialist planning that was developed in Vienna by von Mises and others in the 1920s and also from the common heritage of Kantian idealism which Viennese economics had shared with other sections of German thought. From these beginnings Hayek developed: first, a theory of knowledge and information, and then one of social progress. This said: useful developments depend on the actions of individuals at the local level. Social progress is about being in the right place at the right time, and fitting things together in a very local and informal way. Little good comes out of central planning at the centre of society. There is a subjectivist tinge to his thought: he believes that individuals impose their own meanings on the world and he is very suspicious of abstractions such as 'society' and 'social justice'.

Now starting from these general ideas Hayek developed over five decades and in four different countries a series of implications which follow from them. Best known, early on, there is the critique of central planning set out in *The Road to Serfdom,* but more entertainingly, I think, in *The Counter-Revolution of Science.* There was a development of themes for the political order, and the drawing out of implications for the

17

political order in what was called at the time the 'magnificent dinosaur' of the *Constitution of Liberty*: a dinosaur that is revived and is trumpeting around the world. These are the definitions of freedom and coercion. Freedom is negative freedom, the absence of coercion of the will of one person by another. Rights are limited to those rights acquired by slaves when emancipated in classical times. So rights are about the right of free movement and the right to own property; there are *no* social or economic or human rights alongside those basic rights.

More recently Hayek has developed a particular approach to law, in which he praises the idea of limited general rules, known in advance, and contrasts it with the *ad hoc* ruling of bodies like the CRE which attempt to come in after the event to influence decisions. So what is the implication or inference for race relations that can be drawn from his thought? I think he would say that if you have a free society, with diversity and individual choice groups that are discriminated against at one point in time will work out their own salvation. Central agencies attempting to define such difficult concepts as discrimination or to decide *ex post facto* on the fairness of particular actions of individuals will certainly do much more harm than good. In fact it would be a bootstrap approach to discrimination. Let the social order take its own course and people will find their own salvation.

My critique of Hayek, in the book I recently published on the New Right's economics, concentrated on his neglect of private coercion. There is a view implicit in much of Hayek and Friedman's thought that coercion has emerged from government action. Although Hayek has, I think, a greater sense of civil society, not just of government and markets, he does neglect the possibility of coercion by groups, individuals, religious factions and so on. He also neglects psychological coercion. I find it very difficult to fit together the subjectivism of Hayek with his highly physical and material view of freedom and coercion. He talks about physical control of the will, or physical alteration of the will, as if that were the only way freedom could be invaded. That is hard to fit in with his highly subjectivist view of life. And above all I think he neglects the influence of tyranny of opinion. Like many economists, Hayek has read Adam Smith: like very few of them he has also read Hume, but he has not read the critical passages of Hume, I think, when he talks about the importance of opinion in dominating government actions. And he does not seem to have read the work which towers over modern writings of the New Right: de Tocqueville's *Democracy in America*. There is not much there which is not in *The Modern Economics of Politics*. And de Tocqueville had a very real sense of government responding to trends in opinion rather than being an independent force in itself. So that would be the Hayekian approach to race relations.

Friedman has written a great deal about race relations, and the particular propositions are as follows. Firstly, there is the general one that liberties of speech, and diversity and freedom for individuals, depend on free markets. Political collectivism will lead to tyranny. Following from that is the sub-proposition that such progress as black people have made in the US (and he admits that they have faced special difficulties), have been made through the market, and their right to own property, rather than because of government action. He has also developed a critique of fair employment practices law. They are an unfair way of dealing with discrimination because the discriminator (the employer or the store-owner) is simply reflecting customer opinion. It is unfair to make the discriminator the scapegoat for wider social attitudes which he is simply reflecting. Basically Friedman is prepared to leave markets and persuasion to deal with discrimination. He took over, without developing it fully, the Beckerian approach which sees discrimination as involving an economic cost. An employer who discriminates in not hiring an efficient worker because he is black will suffer a cost because of that. Friedman is in effect saying that once employers realise they are suffering this cost, they will go in there and hire the Gujerati building worker and discrimination will wither away. And he also recommended persuasion in a free society, though my experience as a civil rights worker in Mississippi in the 1960s suggests that the power of persuasion there would have been quite limited.

Those were early views developed in *Capitalism and Freedom*. Recently he has concentrated more on the role of public monopoly services and a critique of them for reducing the chances of blacks to make gains through markets. He has always accepted that, where the choice is between enforced integration and enforced segregation in the context of a monopoly school system, then the least worst option is enforced integration. But, he says, a much better option would be a voucher system in which blacks and whites could decide whether to go to mixed schools or to black or white schools. And he has developed a strong critique both of education and of the social security system in the US. The social security system, he says, is a way of transferring income from black people who are in the labour force, who start young paying contributions and then die young. They are the losers, while people who enter the labour force late — graduates and those who spend many years living in Florida in retirement — are the gainers from the social security system. There are similar gains and losses in education.

I believe that Friedman raises some empirical issues which deserve far more attention from people involved in race relations. The first is; what has been the relative importance of markets, as against public services, in bringing about both discrimination and also some approach to equality? I spent some time as Chairman of a Housing Committee in the London Borough of Camden and I did what I could. We set up what was I think, at the time the only really effective system for trying to detect and root out the harassment of Asian tenants on council estates. There is no doubt that there was a major problem of intimidation and violence on council estates, and one has to ask what is the score of the public services as against owner occupation in promoting equal opportunities? These are empirical issues. One can ask about young West Indians, how well do they do in the first ten or fifteen years in the labour market compared with their experience at school? There have been 'Friedman' effects certainly, for Asian building workers. I know from my friends in the Kenyan Asian community that fifteen years ago, when a Kenyan Asian building worker approached a site in central London, he would be told 'No luck', 'Get off'. Now he would be welcomed and waved onto the site because it is known that his productivity is very high. And that is an example of a Friedman process at work, and we need much more evidence about relative productivities and how they interact with discrimination against various groups.

Besides those particular empirical issues which grow from Friedman's work, I think there are also some wider issues about the way the case for equality and against discrimination has been made. This case has been one item in an ideological approach. That is to say, those who are in favour of race relations legislation have been people who think extension of state action in almost any sphere is a good thing. And the whole approach to race in Britain and America has got identified with the political left. Yet I believe that there is a strong case for action to promote equality in other terms, such as freedom of access to markets and freedom of exchange. This could be a more powerful and acceptable case in an increasingly marketised environment. The more collectivist case, emphasising the role of public employment and public action in various ways may need expanding against a background of declining collectivism in society. So I think serious attention should be given to the possibility of a market-based case for anti-discrimination policies, and for a critique of discrimination which concentrates on how it reduces exchange possibilities and introduces irrelevant, harmful considerations into exchange possibilities. Friedman has set a challenge, I think, to everybody who is interested in equality.

His record on issues such as civil liberties is not as bad as is generally thought. For example, he opposed the draft for many years on the grounds of its coercive effects. He also opposed strongly, on libertarian grounds, the McCarthyite blacklist of producers and script-writers in Hollywood in the early 1950s, at a time when that was not a popular move to make. He opposes fair employment practices legislation on similar libertarian grounds. But I believe, without necessarily sharing all his views, that there is a market case than can be made for action to reduce discrimination, and that in the kind of environment into which western societies are moving we should be trying to develop that case much more.

Answers to questions

Q. I think the point about using the market to extend opportunities and so get rid of discrimination, has been extremely well taken. But I don't really see that as an alternative to the kinds of intervention that you have to make through other processes of State or legal action.

A. I don't disagree that there is a need for action on both sides but, given the general trend of opinion, there is a need to diversify the approach a bit, compared with what went over well in the more corporatist 1960s and 1970s. I think the question of what is free exchange, and fairness, in transactions and markets is a very important one, that needs a lot more discussion.

Q. There are two ideas which need to be kept very distinct even though they are verbal formulations that are very similar. They are the ideas of, on the one hand, getting rid of discrimination in the market, which we must all be in favour of and the importance of which socialists and leftists may have depreciated and the idea of using the market to get rid of discrimination, which is a quite different idea. Using the market as a means of ending discrimination seems to me to confuse discrimination with advancing the interests of particular sets of people within minorities.

A. Well, for example in the housing market, minorities have been denied access to building society funds in many areas in the past, and this has involved a huge cost for them in that they had to borrow the money elsewhere. It has involved restrictions on freedom of movement which have affected their access to the labour market and therefore their chances of accumulating assets, gaining the job experience and so on. So it is difficult to see how there can be real equality unless minority groups have access to the same range of economic and social processes which have created some degree of greater equality for the host community.

Q. Aren't we discussing this problem in unduly narrow terms as if discrimination were the whole problem? The reason for the law and the CRE is not simply discrimination but injustice and inequality for groups of people based on totally irrational grounds. All the law says is that there are certain steps the State can take which would help to mitigate this. We started this discussion by discussing what Hayek and Friedman said: roughly that if you leave racial injustice alone it will cure itself. Now it isn't either left-wing or right-wing to say they are wrong. You can say empirically history shows this is untrue. So I don't see why we should be

put into an ideological strait-jacket or ask whether the market can or cannot do it by itself.

A. Hayek and Friedman would argue that the State has not been very effective in providing opportunities and reducing inequality for minority groups like Jews in the United States and the Irish in Britain but that the market has been effective.

Roger Scruton and Neo-conservatism

Alan Ryan

In contrast to the libertarian and free market thesis of the 'neo-liberals' are the ideas of 'neo-conservatives' who, far from minimising the role of the State, exalt it above the individual. This school of thought finds expression in the *Salisbury Review* and other journals with a small circulation, but has achieved enormous influence through the daily press. Alan Ryan, Fellow of New College Oxford, looks at the work of Roger Scruton, and asks how new the new conservatism really is.

I shall begin with a small typology: then I shall say a bit about Roger Scruton's view of the universe and its impact on views about race, or on xenophobia in general. The world divides into three classes of persons for the purpose of my argument. The main enemy of *all* the people who are called members of the New Right are the welfare state liberals. There is a sense in which 'real radicals' are thought to be kindred spirits and therefore not too bad. Welfare state liberalism is the doctrine that the rights which people have in society rule out the enforcement by the State of particular moral perspectives and religious allegiances, but do not guarantee the sanctity of private property. In other words the State has the discretion to alter rules about ownership and the generation of income, but it does not have discretion to enforce any particular moral view of the world. This is why anti-discrimination policies are part of the welfare state liberal tool kit: such policies stop people being victimised by the moral prejudices of other people in their society. And because property is not sacred, discrimination cannot hide behind it.

The libertarian in the American sense (not the sense that is attached to the lunatic fringe like the Federation of Conservative Students) shares the welfare state liberal view that the State has no right to enforce any particular moral perspective, but libertarians go on to say that private property *is* sacred. Indeed the libertarian prohibition on enforcement of a particular moral perspective is held to be a deduction from the sanctity of private property. We are inviolable, because we have a property in ourselves. *That* libertarian view — Nozick's and Rothbard's — is actually detested by genuine conservatives in this country and in general. People like Hayek whose sympathies are libertarian (with qualifications because

23

of the importance of tradition) object very strongly to being called conservatives precisely because they see themselves as in that liberal camp. The truly conservative view, of which Scruton is the most articulate, literate defender is that the first position to which the welfare State liberal is attached — that the State has no business enforcing any particular moral perspective on the world — is just wrong, perniciously wrong, and from it all sorts of other vices flow. The whole view of the nature of rights, of law, of tradition, of the nature of the State on which that basic liberal perception rests, is on this view just wrong. Contrary to the libertarian view, private property is not sacrosanct in the sense of being immune to any amount of legal tinkering by the State. But, contrary to the liberal view, it is *almost* sacred. To understand the grounds of private property is to understand that it must have a nearly sacred status in a stable society; many inequalities and many discriminatory practices simply have to be accepted as the price of maintaining this nearly sacred institution. It is not sacrosanct for the reasons Nozick, or anyone of that kind, would want to come up with. It is sacred for culturally rich reasons which I should now explain.

But first it is worth saying something about the kind of arguments that Scruton thinks politics involve. I am not referring to what appears in the *Salisbury Review*, or the *Times* on Tuesdays but the doctrine according to Scruton in his articulate philosophical moments.

Arguing about politics he says, comes in three layers. The ultimate philosophical position one takes is not directly political. That is to say, the ultimate philosophical view of the world on which one's political views are premissed is not itself part of the political argument, though that ultimate philosophical position must frame the arguments that controversialists come up with. Your ultimate philosophical commitment provides a methodological framework for political arguments but does not directly determine them. Scruton's book on *The Meaning of Conservatism* is not, therefore, a *philosophical* book. It is a book written at the second layer or level of argument, an exercise in dogmatics. What 'dogmatics' is, is the argued defence of a political outlook which is not rationalisable in a complete or comprehensive way. *No* political position can be rationalised in any complete or comprehensive way, and persons who think that political outlooks can be so rationalised are, as de Maistre said a long time ago, a menace to polite society. All they succeed in doing is destabilising the attachment of the plain man to his society: as de Maistre said 'They are the people who let slip the leash of a tiger'.

Particular political policies and proposals belong at the bottom of the pyramid and are the day to day business of politicians and people who write in the newspapers. (So bright ideas like repatriating recent immigrants and their descendants belong at the bottom of the heap and not in a work of dogmatics like *The Meaning of Conservatism*.)

24

This means that though Scruton is in the Hegelian tradition *The Meaning of Conservatism* is not quite like *The Philosophy of Right*. The *Philosophy of Right* operates in a grey area somewhere between philosophy and dogmatics, thus construed. But it is like Hegel, and the obvious tradition it belongs in is the Hegelian tradition, because it makes our actual dealings with the world the test of ethical significance. That is to say, a rock bottom presumption is that it is the actual allegiances and attachments of the people you find around you (which are not themselves based on articulate ideas) that constrain political writers; the job of the theorist is to show the implicit rationale of these not entirely articulate ideas. As Hegel says the task is to show 'what the state is, not what it ought to be'. Dogmatics does not propose ideals; it's about describing the world in such a way that people reinforce their attachments to the world as it is. And if you ask, 'Complete with all its imperfections?' the reply is 'Yes, complete with all its imperfections'.

This means that the prime target of attack is the liberal reformer. Marxists on the one hand and blunt class warriors on the other operate, as far as Scruton is concerned, on the right terrain. Politics can take a good deal of class conflict. It can absorb different groups contending for power over other groups, contending for economic and political advantage. Politics must have a place for a legitimate struggle between the haves and the have-nots, and this struggle can take place in essentially non-grudge-bearing ways. I think myself that by now this view has become a degenerate romanticism. But it is, at all events, a view which appears to be held by Scruton.

The real monster, on this view, is the liberal rationalist because the liberal rationalist spends all his time looking at institutions asking 'Why do we do it this way, couldn't we do it some better way?' It is the desire for constant improvement, for tinkering, and making things work better that causes all the trouble. And therefore it is the liberal reformer, the person who wants to keep on examining the roots of the organic growth that constitutes society, who is the real menace.

Scruton thinks that, if his book is successful, what it achieves is to change the onus of proof. The liberal believes that the burden of proof is on those who want to maintain the present in the face of the proposition that some other way of doing things would be better. Scruton wants to switch the argument round so that the burden of proof is on those who want to disturb things. You don't have to show that what we have got is the best of all possible worlds; all you have to show is that this is the world we have indeed got. And the onus of proof therefore is on the disturbers.

This view is deeply and almost venomously anti-Nozickian, anti-Rawlsian, anti any kind of individualistic, historical, abstracting mode of argument. It stands on a fundamentally Hegelian ground, namely that individuals are the consequence of social organisation not the premisses of it. Nozick and Rawls both construct a model of society and our obligations to each other *after* asking what kind of deals would we, person by person, have let ourselves in for had we started off in the state of nature? This reflects a moral individualism to which Scruton is quite attached but only in a particular way. I'll explain in a moment why only in that way, and only 'quite attached'. What Scruton thinks, in a Hegelian way, is that although individualism reflects a valuable strand of the western moral tradition it does so in a fundamentally misleading manner. The non-misleading way is to understand acceptable individualism as the product of, and only sustainable by, a certain kind of society, namely a deeply conservative one.

So Scruton sometimes looks as if he is arguing, like Michael Oakeshott, that because it developed a certain kind of legal and parliamentary framework, our society generated scope for individual freedom and room for action by individuals but only by preserving institutions to which people were attached for traditional reasons. They had grown up knowing how to work them, and, having grown up knowing how to work them, could lead individually varied and satisfying existences on the strength of these institutions.

I think, (though people quarrel about this) that Oakeshott is in fact much more of an individualist and liberal than Scruton is. Scruton is really hostile to almost all claims on behalf of individual freedom because his great attachment is to the family. Nozick's view of the world is peculiar because Nozick's own feelings are exceedingly sentimental, and based on close Jewish communities of a long ago New York. Yet Nozick supposes that we are parachuted into the world free, white, unattached, 22, and frightfully clever, while Scruton, who exemplifies upwardly socially mobile individualism by temperament, is doctrinally deeply attached to the family. It is families rather than individuals that carry the weight of the story. Scruton says in the coda to the second edition that it's a third-person and sociological doctrine in the sense that it always asks the question 'How does that group or tribe' (the word he uses) 'keep its way of life going?' It does not ask the first-person question, 'Does it violate *my* rights?'

Given that framework — group-orientated, tradition-centred, family-based and so on — there is a pressure towards the kind of conservatism he comes up with. But you do not *have* to get that kind of conservatism out of that framework. Hegel, I think was rather more liberal than Scruton, Oakeshott certainly is much more liberal than Scruton.

Seven fundamental propositions comes out of all this. Proposition one: there are no natural rights and one shouldn't start from the position that individuals have them. Certainly society ought to give people rights, and ought to maintain the rule of law. But the existence of rights and the rule of law is a social achievement, which depends on maintaining certain institutions, such as an independent judiciary. (This of course is a way of thumbing his nose at the liberals because they and the Left will want habitually to tinker with the judiciary for the sake of making sure that the law gives people their natural rights. Someone like Ronnie Dworkin is standing fair and square in front of Scruton's cannon because his quasi-natural rights theory puts pressure on the behaviour of the judges). Scruton's view says that the price of the rule of law is an independent judiciary resistant to that kind of claim. If you want the rule of law you must have judicial independence, which, no doubt, leaves you vulnerable to the prejudices of upper-middle-class old men but that is the price you inescapably pay.

Proposition two: the State may do absolutely anything and nobody has any ultimate rights against it. So if, for example, you claim that the State has no right to torture people Scruton will get off the bus. *In extremis,* there is nothing that the State may not do. This is really only a fierce version of *Salus populi suprema lex* but what Scruton is doing is distancing his kind of conservatism from knock-kneed liberalism. Of course, says Scruton cheerfully, the State, if it is prudent, will not ill-treat its own inhabitants because if it does their allegiance is bound to fizzle out. In general the State must do all those things that liberals think it ought to do. But this is not to say that the State has no right to go far beyond that *in extremis*. This leads on to a defence of *raison d'e tat,* famous from Hegel's well-known view that history is a slaughter bench, and equally visible in Scruton.

Thirdly, socialism is absolutely out. People need private property because they need privacy. People come into the world in all sorts of different shapes, sizes, tastes, interests and the rest of it, and unless you have private property you cannot have quirks of character, or the stability of family life, or the scope for action that individuals need if they are to turn out to be real human beings. Any attempt to deprive them of such an environment will result in disaster. This is not however a defence of *laissez-faire*. Since there are no natural rights, the State *can* do anything: it *can* tinker with the rules about property as much as it likes. This argument holds that something close to *laissez-faire* is likely to be desirable. It defends a kind of moderated capitalism, and it certainly says that the attempt to enforce social justice, or to interfere a great deal, will result in greater evils than it suppresses. But it does not defend capitalism in a Nozickian way.

Fourth, society must offer people, and ensure that they can find, kinds of work which will allow them to establish some kind of identity in the world. The defence of property and work is that work is not what Marx called alienated labour; work allows people to see their own achievements in the world. This is very like Hannah Arendt; but when

27

Scruton defends Mrs Thatcher and glories in the Falklands campaign he is notably silent about the fact that several million people cannot find work that would allow them to express themselves and their capabilities adequately in their daily lives. In a work of dogmatics, as opposed to mere party politics, it is a disgraceful silence.

Fifthly, there is no right to private moral views. Society sets, and must set, moral standards by tradition, and must rely upon a degree of control which would be deplored by Mill, Nozick and any liberal. The Nozickian view is that, since my body is mine, I can ingest anything I like and share its potentialities with anyone of any sex or any inclinations I like. But society has to turn out people who can work in that society; its standards have to be bolted into the environment in such a way that anyone not living up to them is ruled out of the social 'game'.

Sixthly, we must then allow people the right to exclude others from sharing their own existences with them, because otherwise one can't maintain the environment in which parents can train their children in appropriate ways. The price of this is inescapably some degree of xenophobia or racism. The conclusion is that we should not try to force upon people a degree of accommodation to other people's strangenesses and oddnesses that they cannot manage. They will be less xenophobic if not pressed too hard.

Seventhly, politics is not about achieving ideals. Ultimate ideals are undiscussable. There is a wonderful paragraph in *The Meaning of Conservatism* which says that when we have come to the end of the book we have reached the realm about which one cannot talk. Ultimate ideals are simply beyond discussion. There is a realm of attachments left to literature, art and perhaps to philosophy. Politics is not about these things; politics is about preserving society as we've got it.

Unlike Gerald Cohen, who has virtuously abstained from saying what he thought of his target, I shall make a couple of comments. First the connection between the framework and the details in this way of talking about politics cannot be tight. There is no way in which you can make the arguments deductive. All you can claim is that a certain way of arguing is forced upon you. So, for example, if you are a liberal of a Hegelian kind then you have got to argue for the potentialities of the community to enlarge people's freedom. Scruton will not do this, but people like TH Green used to, and Michael Walzer still does. The framework does not *dictate* conservatism. But it dictates that, if you are going to be a liberal, you must be a communitarian liberal, not a natural rights liberal.

Two large questions and a footnote question are raised by this. The first large question is whether such a broadly Hegelian picture makes any sense when Hegel's own view of history as the march of reason is removed. Scruton's Hegelianism is an act of will. Hegel thought that history was under the control of reason and that you could put up with the irrationalities of the world as we found it, because they were subsumed under a larger rationality. In Scruton, we have our noses rubbed in the irrationalities. That is a large difference, and the question, what is left once the Hegelian rationalism goes, is decidedly awkward.

The second large question (which I am not going to answer) is why we have to follow Scruton rather than Mill. Mill agreed that the individual whose development he desired was the product of society, not its premiss, and then explained how society might create him. There seems no reason why merely agreeing that the individual is a social not a natural creation should land us in an irrationalist conservatism. Try as I might, I'm damned if I can see an argument for it.

There is a footnote to this question. Given that the Scruton picture was produced for the first time in 1979 and was written in the fading days of the Callaghan regime; is this view of the world tolerable in opposition but intolerable when it becomes triumphalist after 1983? I ask this for the following boring reason, which is that the preface to the new edition of *The Meaning of Conservatism* talks a certain amount of nonsense about the Falklands war, and rejoices in the way the British set out to fight merely for the sake of kith and kin. This is what you might call the slide from *Times* Toryism to *Sun* Toryism. The milder doctrine says: you must not put too much pressure on families or groups; if you are going to have open-door immigration, you should not be surprised if the natives occasionally get restive when a lot of newcomers turn up next door, and so forth. The triumphalist version says, 'Here is ours, it's ours; it can only be ours at all if it absolutely *is* ours and we are going to slam the bloody door and people can lump it.' The milder doctrine was used critically against the people in charge, and the triumphalist version is used when you yourself are in charge. I myself think that the triumphalist version is just disgusting. Since Scruton's is after all a work of dogmatics not of philosophy, we are seemingly excused elaborate philosophical reasons for saying it is disgusting; I simply observe that the frame of mind on this evidence is not a nice frame of mind.

Answers to questions

Q. I think that one can't really look at Scruton only in terms of *The Meaning of Conservatism* but in terms of the whole role of the *Times* and the *Sun* and the way in which this particular kind of neo-conservatism has now become the establishment in New Printing House Square. The other thing is that Scruton, through the *Salisbury Review*, has brought together an extraordinary band of people who differ fundamentally. Not all of them belong to the New Right. Some of them belong to quite an old Right. He has created a platform for Enoch Powell, Ray Honeyford, old liturgy people within the Church of England and the Roman Communion, people of a variety of views, brought together very much by the Falklands spirit and

the new nationalism. This is of direct relevance to race, as one can see if one looks at John Casey's articles about how black people are an essentially alien force in a sense that the Falkland islanders are not. And so I find Scruton very worrying, not simply in himself, but in the role he plays.

A. I have two views about that. One is that you are absolutely right, and there is a sinister side because people are persuaded that their paranoid reactions are all right. There is a fudge in the whole business, because two persons are always visible. One is 'I'm really a philosopher and not engaged in the hurly burly', but the other side is simply vituperation and contempt for everybody within sight, and that is pretty much saloon bar politics. But one cheering thought is that on a longer historical perspective its not as bad as you might think. If you go back to the things that conservatives habitually said in the 1920s, it is striking that we have for the last 30 odd years, as a result of the Second World War, taken for granted a level of decency in arguing about politics that nobody took for granted before the second world war. One thing the *Salisbury Review* skirts is anti-semitism. In the 1920s they wouldn't have flinched. They would have cheerfully talked about Jew financiers and kikes. In that sense then it isn't quite as shocking as we now tend to feel it partly because we've had a good run. It doesn't make it any nicer.

Q. But nevertheless couldn't Ken Leech's comment be generalised in another way, to suggest that the Scruton phenomenon can serve as a reminder to academic philosophers and theologians of something which I think people in both these trades have often forgotten, and that is, that all our discourses are in fact practical instruments of power?

A. That's a very large question. That point operates at two levels. There is the public prints level — namely, why are people on the other side timid about rolling up their sleeves and piling in? — and it is true they are timid. After Christmas one of the Fabian philosophy group was offered Scruton's slot for a couple of weeks and couldn't manage to write anything in 450 words that he wanted to put there. That flinching seems to me a practical version of your question. The other point, that all our discourses are about power — it seems to me that in the last 30 years they haven't been; we've been let off the hook. We have been allowed to operate in an ivory tower, but it may well get rougher from now on.

Q. I don't understand how one can reconcile the sort of nationalism you have been talking about with a defence of *laissez-faire* economics. Surely a free market implies free movement of labour, and therefore open immigration? You say Scruton defends a kind of moderated capitalism. But someone like Enoch Powell seems to find no difficulty in combining straight capitalism with a ban on immigration. How is it done?

A. My own view about this is that the Enoch Powell view of the world is not incoherent. A lot of people ask how one can run the Powell line about gung-ho *laissez-faire* in economics but nationalism in one's politics. How can you spend your time doing cost benefit analysis about everything except about whether its worth keeping the Falkland Islands? It's like everything else in this doctrine; you pick your favourite bits and insulate them from the rest of the story. People who are more intellectually sober than I'm prone to be about politics, think that people like Nozick are serious people because they've got a story that runs right the way down from one end to the other. In Nozick's world, you cope with Russia by not selling them computers, not by inventing star wars and wasting money left, right and centre. But Enoch Powell, Mrs. Thatcher and Scruton all hold the view that it is the combination of *laissez-faire* and nationalism that you put your shirt on. You can draw lines in different places, but essentially hostility to immigration is central to the story because proposition one is, 'The show doesn't get off the road unless *we* are *us*'. Intellectuals are prone to produce ideal pictures, and come out looking nastier than the practical politicians. The intellectuals say it would make perfectly good sense and it wouldn't violate anybody's real rights if you chucked all the newcomers out again. Politicians are much more likely in practice to want a quiet life. This neo-conservatism is quite like traditional conservatism. If you go back to the 1920s you can find people behaving just like this. And think of Disraeli. The Tory Left goes on about Disraeli being the great 'one nation' person, but he believed straightforwardly in *laissez-faire* everywhere and nationalism to keep the chaps happy. What *is* true is that we have now got an activist version of all this in a way which we didn't have. It is more gung-ho because it thinks it's got to roll back the tide of the liberal and reformers. The doctrine is not so different.

The 'New Right' and the Politics of Nationhood
Bhikhu Parekh

Bhikhu Parekh, Professor of Politics at Hull University and Deputy Chairman of the Commission for Racial Equality, analyses the views on nationality, race and the State promulgated by a number of writers including John Casey, Enoch Powell, Peregrine Worsthorne, Roger Scruton and Alfred Sherman. He shows how these theories have had direct effects in the United Kingdom on attitudes and policies towards racial minorities, and argues an alternative theory of the nature of the State and the nation.

The term 'New Right' began to gain currency in Britain at about the same time as the term 'New Left', but has proved more durable. For several reasons it is of questionable value. First, it was coined and given currency because of the feeling that over the past few decades, the Right had acquired novel features that entitled it to be called the New Right. A careful examination of the history of conservatism would show that the allegedly new features are not really all that new. Second, which is closely related to the first, those described as belonging to the New Right have generally rejected the description on the ground that the ideas they espouse have always belonged to the dominant strand within the conservative tradition and represent the old and 'authentic' Right. Third, in describing a body of beliefs as the New Right, we imply that they are confined to those belonging to the Right or that the Right is particularly sympathetic to them. Neither proposition is true. Some of these beliefs are shared by the Left as well and informed the policies pursued by successive Labour governments in the sixties and seventies. Nor is it true that the Right is necessarily attracted to these beliefs. Indeed, a fairly powerful critique of the New Right is provided in the writings of Michael Oakeshott, an important conservative thinker. For these and other reasons I shall avoid the term New Right.

I

I intend in this paper to concentrate on a manner of thinking about politics that has become quite dominant during the past few years.

33

Although it is by no means confined to them, it has so far been articulated and openly avowed by such conservative writers as Enoch Powell, Roger Scruton, John Casey, Maurice Cowling, Peregrine Worsthorne and Alfred Sherman and, at a different level, by Mrs Thatcher and some of her parliamentary colleagues. These individuals do, no doubt, take divergent views on several substantive questions. However they all share a common perspective on and a common way of analysing and defining British political life. Basically they are all agreed upon the following three propositions.

First, Britain has been in a state of decline almost since the end of the Second World War. Second the decline is at several levels, of which the economic, the moral and the political are the most important. The economic decline is taken to consist in low productivity, the narrowing of the manufacturing base, the unfavourable balance of payments and so on, and at a deeper level in the lack of initiative and enterprise and a low view of the entrepreneurial and commercial culture. The moral decline, which is closely related to the economic, is taken to consist in the loss of such economically crucial moral virtues as thrift, hard work, self-discipline, willigness to suffer poverty rather than accept the indignity of charity, standing on one's own feet, initiative, absence of jealousy at others' opulence and a sense of personal responsibility. It is contended that these virtues, which had made Britain the strongest industrial nation and the greatest imperial power in the world in the nineteenth century, are being systematically undermined by the liberal consensus institutionalised in the permissive and over-protective welfare state. As for the political decline, it is taken to consist in the confusion or loss of national identity. a weakening of the sense of patriotism and the decline of public culture and spirit.

Third, Britain's decline can only be arrested by means of a well co-ordinated radical strategy on each of the three fronts. The economic strategy consists, among other things, in strengthening the forces of the market, encouraging vigorous competition, minimising government intervention, reducing public expenditure and curtailing the services provided by the state. The moral strategy consists in strengthening the family, restoring the structure of authority and nurturing the culture of discipline in all walks of life, encouraging women to stay at home to mind the family, requiring the schools to transmit Victorian moral values and fighting the moral flabbiness of the permissive society. The political strategy consists in fostering a clear sense of national identity based on the unity of 'stock', a common public culture and a strong spirit of patriotism based on a sense of 'kinship'.

It is this curious and unstable combination of the market mechanism, moral authoritarianism and the racially based theory of national identity that characterises most of the writers under consideration. No doubt, different writers give pride of place to different elements and relate them differently. However they are all agreed that a satisfactory analysis and solution of Britain's problems is only to be found within the framework of the three propositions sketched above. Since I am interested in their views on the place of black communities in Britain, I shall concentrate on their theory of national identity.

II

For the writers we are discussing, every modern State is inherently fragile and subject to constant internal and external threats to its existence. In order to maintain itself as a stable entity vigorously pursuing its interests in a hostile world, it must develop a strong sense of unity. The sense of unity, we are told, is grounded in a strong sense of nationality or nationhood, defined as an 'instinctive' feeling of belonging to a common group and being bound to it by sentiments of affection, piety, collective pride and loyalty constantly murtured by the inherently inarticulate pool of tacit understanding and unspoken sympathies which marks out the group from the others. It is this sense of nationality, the unity of sentiment and feeling that gives the State a moral and emotional depth and constitutes an unshakable basis of its internal unity.

It is argued that the unity of sentiment and feeling is complex and elusive. It cannot be reduced to such things as long settlement in one place, shared religion and culture, and willingness to acknowledge common authority. The Greeks under the Turkish rule had most of these, and yet did not share with them a sense of nationality. Conversely the Jews of the Diaspora, who had none of these, were nevertheless united by the deepest ties of sentiment and loyalty. The unity of sentiment, we are told, grows out of shared history, customs, way of life and, above all, a sense of belonging to a common 'kind' or 'kinship'. Although this much-used and crucial but never clearly defined term is used in several senses, it is generally given a biological or at least an ethnic connotation. It is argued or more often simply assumed that the feeling of kinship cannot be acquired or inculcated; it is based on the unity of 'stock', 'race' or 'kind', and one either has it or lacks it by virtue of birth. As John Casey puts it a sense of nationality or patriotism is a matter of 'feeling for, loyalty to people of one's own kind'. He goes on, 'There is no way of understanding English patriotism that averts its eyes from the fact that it has at its centre a feeling for persons of one's own kind'. For Roger Scruton, it implies 'a desire for the company of one's kind'. In all these writers the term 'kind' means stock or race, and defines the boundary of kinship.

For Powell, Casey, Scruton and others, a nation, a community bound together by a deep sense of kinship, is the highest unit of moral and political life. One cannot be moral except against the background of mutual trust and instinctive loyalties, and these are only possible within a national community. Such political virtues as patriotism, honour and the pursuit of public interest come easily and indeed are only possible when the community is not an impersonal legal abstraction but a living reality. In other words, only the nation can give content and energy to moral and political life. As Casey puts it, the 'moral life finds its fulfilment only in an actual historical human community and above all in a nation-state'. One may at best be moral but never ethical, that is, practise *Moralität* but never *Sittlechkeit* in one's relations with those outside one's nation. Alfred Sherman puts the point well: 'national consciousness is the sheet-anchor for the unconditional loyalties and acceptance of duties and responsibilities based on personal identification with the national community, which underlie civic duty and patriotism'. Since the nation is taken to define the bounds of loyalties, Sherman, Powell and others reject the very concept of obligations to mankind in general.

It is in terms of the unity of the British stock that these writers analyse the Anglo-Argentinian war over the Falklands and the current situation in Northern Ireland. Britain was right to go to war with Argentina, not because the abstract principle of self-determination was at stake, nor because aggression should not be the basis of relations between States, but because the Falklanders were 'British by every conceivable test, by language, custom and race', and had a claim to Britain's support. Indeed, thanks to the strong feeling of kinship, the British people spontaneously felt a deep and passionate sense of concern for their aggrieved kinsmen and rushed to their defence. For similar reasons the British people must and indeed want to maintain the existing links with Northern Ireland, the bulk of whose inhabitants are tied to them by 'race and religion'.

It is in the context of this theory of national unity that these writers analyse the presence of black communities in Britain. As usual the latter are divided into the West Indians and Asians, and different arguments are advanced against each. The West Indians, we are told, define themselves in terms of colour, their internal bond of solidarity and mark of separation from the British society. They have a sense of identity and interests different in their eyes from those of the majority. They do not wish to be part of British society nor will the latter ever accept them as one. They harbour deep resentment against British society, hate all authority including and especially that of the police, the teachers and Parliament, are inherently rebellious and anarchic, and hold values wholly at variance with Britain's. For Casey they simply cannot form part of 'our' group or belong to 'our' kind, for their behaviour outrages 'our' sense of what English life should be like and how the English should behave towards a duly constituted authority. Indeed, says Casey, they are uncivilised and their conduct 'offends' our 'sense of what is civilised behaviour'.

36

As for the Asians, they are said to be intelligent, industrious, peaceable, and possessing many of the domestic virtues prized by the British. However they are deeply attached to their languages and customs, have a 'profoundly' different culture from Britain's, are only loyal to the Indian sub-Continent and constitute an 'alien wedge'. Robert Taylor, MP, is kind enough to give an example of the inassimilable nature of the Asians. Referring to an Asian family, he observes:

> The family was insistent that their daughter should marry an Indian from the Indian sub-Continent. That is more racialist than any other action one can think of, because it is a rejection of other races and customs and a rejection of our society's customs.

The black communities, then, cannot form part of the British nation. They are not just foreign, but 'alien' and hostile. They do not 'instinctively' identify themselves with Britain, and the British 'instinctively' recognise them as belonging to a different kind of stock. Peregrine Worsthorne seems to think they might all be fifth columnists 'whose allegiance may be with the enemies of the West,[1] namely the Third World'. In his view 'a large number of them do not want to stop hating this country, let alone start to love it'.[2] For Powell, Casey and Sherman their presence erodes the unity of national sentiment and subverts Britain's sense of nationhood. The British feel deeply threatened by them and fear for their unity and integrity as a nation. They cannot be blamed for feeling this way for it is inherent in 'human nature' to wish to live with men and women of one's kind. Britain is the 'natural home' of the people of British stock, just as India is that of the Indians and Jamaica of the Jamaicans. Deep and irresoluble tensions are bound to be generated when British doors are thrown open to people of different races, and the 'hospitable' British nature is subjected to intolerable pressures. Enoch Powell remarks:

> The disruption of the homogeneous we, which forms the essential basis of our parliamentary democracy and, therefore, of our liberties, is now approaching the point at which the political mechanisms of a 'divided community' takes charge and begin to operate autonomously.

John Stokes, MP, complains about the 'rape of the English race' and the 'violation of the rights' of the English people, and observes:

> I came here only six years ago, I came to help my country, I have seen my task as that of trying to keep all that is best in England and to be able to hand on to my children, as my father handed on to me, a country to be proud of, a homogeneous nation sharing the same faith, history and background. I must make it clear that I do not blame the immigrants for coming — they came largely for the money — but I blame those who encouraged and still encourage them.

Since the black minorities form an alien wedge, these writers advocate a threefold strategy. First, under no circumstances should the number of blacks be allowed to increase. There is therefore to be a complete embargo on black immigration. The whites must, of course, remain free to enter Britain, and the British free to emigrate abroad, including the Third World countries. Second, every attempt should be made to prevent or at least delay the entry of the wives and children of black British citizens, so that they may get tired or old and never come to Britain or their sponsors may decide to return home. Some of the writers concerned do not actually say this, but it is implicit in their doctrine. Third, some drastic measures should be taken concerning the blacks already settled in Britain. For Peregrine Worsthorne, they should be spread out all over the country and subjected to vigorous cultural assimilation. For Powell, repatriation is the answer. For Casey, the answer lies in retrospectively altering their legal status and turning them into guest workers. All three admit that these are not exactly 'civilised' policies, but insist they are a 'necessity of the state' and required by the British sense of nationhood. Since the maintenance of the nation is the highest and noblest moral ideal such human suffering as might be involved is fully justified. As Casey puts it:

> My defence is this: the state of nationhood is the true state of man, and the danger of ignoring the sentiment of nationhood is actually the danger of the destruction of man as a political animal. Although the courses of action that woud possibly be open to us to preserve the fullest sense of nationhood would be severe, perhaps callous, that alternative political philosophy which sees nothing really profound in the problems posed by mass immigration ... would actually reduce human society to what Burke called 'the gross animal existence of a temporary and perishable nature'.

All these writers are aware that they might be accused of racism. Their reply is either to deny the charge, or to admit it but insist that racism is not immoral. For some, racism stands for a belief in the superiority of some races over others. Since they do not subscribe to the belief and 'only' intend to say that different races represent distinct and exclusive ways of life, they insist that they cannot be accused of racism. Others admit that such a view could be called racism, but insist that it is inherent in human nature or an essential condition of a truly ethical life.

III

The theory of the state outlined above is so obviously incoherent and confused that, had it not found some support in influential circles, one would leave it alone to collapse under the weight of its own contradictions. Let us take its four basic premisses. First, a State is held together by a sense of nationality; that is, the unity of the State is grounded in the unity of the nation. Second, the sense of nationality is only possible among people of a common stock and sharing a feeling of kinship; that is, the unity of the nation is grounded in the unity of stock or kind. Third, the black communities in Britain are incapable of developing affection or loyalty for it and sharing a unity of sentiment with the whites. Fourth, the preservation of nationhood is a supreme moral value and justifies such morally repugnant deeds as their repatriation and forcible assimilation.

Although *prima facie* plausible, the first proposition is clearly untenable. The State does not depend on, and has in fact nothing to do with, a sense of nationality. The United States of America is composed of many nations and nationalities, and yet distinguished by a strong, perhaps too strong a sense of unity. This is also true of almost all modern European states which consist of diverse religious, cultural and ethnic peoples. The modern State is historically unique in that, unlike its predecessors, it has developed an autonomous principle of unity, that is, one located in the very structure of the State rather than in something lying outside or beyond it. The modern State is a product of a long and painful evolution. The bloody religious wars in which fanatical groups struggled to impose their beliefs upon others made it clear that the State must find ways of tolerating religious diversity. With the rise of the spirit of critical inquiry, men began to question the established social order and the inherited moral beliefs, and the State had to learn to accommodate them too. The development of commerce brought together people of different backgrounds, beliefs and ways of life, and the State had to find space for them as well.

In response to all this modern Europe invented the concept of liberty, which had no counterpart in the earlier ages and non-European societies, and evolved a form of organization based upon a delicate balance of the demands of liberty and authority. The State itself was not to subscribe to, let alone to enforce, a specific body of moral, religious or cultural beliefs save those such as the rule of law which were inherent in its structure. Its job was to provide a framework of authority and a body of laws within which individuals and groups were at liberty to live the way they wanted. Unlike the Greek polity based on the unity of *ethnos,* the Roman based on the unity of *cultus* and the medieval polity based on the unity of religion or faith, the modern State is a self-sufficient institution based on the rational unity of its authority. It has a commonly accepted structure of public authority and a set of procedures for taking collectively binding decisions. To be its member is to acknowledge the structure of authority and abide by its laws. Nothing more can or need be expected of its members, for their acknowledgement of the common authority is all that is necessary to maintain its unity.

By its very nature, then, the modern State is a formal institution; its unity lies in its form, not in any substantive identity of race or unity of beliefs. It is therefore able to tolerate diversity in a way its predecessors could not. The earlier forms of political organization felt threatened by religious, moral and cultural diversity. By contrast, the modern State tolerates and welcomes them. The more mature or developed a state, the greater is its capacity to live with and develop unity out of religious, moral, cultural and ethnic diversity. A State that is intolerant of such diversity simply cannot sustain the modern economy, the spirit of rational inquiry or individual liberty. When people live together for a long period of time, they generally tend to develop a common way of life, the love of the land, mutual loyalties, and so on. However even if they do not, the unity of the State, which is independent of these, is not in the least affected. So long as they continue to acknowledge the established authority and abide by the laws, they pose no threat to it. To suggest that the modern State should be based on the unity of nationhood in the hope of returning to a state of primitive simplicity is to understand neither its nature nor its wider context. And to suggest that the unity of Britain must be based on the unity of the British nation is to imply that it is an immature and unsophisticated polity, a ramshackle collection of peoples and institutions that cannot accommodate diversity.

The second proposition is no more persuasive. As we saw, the modern State does not require a sense of nationality or nationhood to sustain its unity. Even if it were granted for the sake of argument that it did, it would not follow that the sense of nationality was possible only among people of a common stock or kind. It is a common historical experience that once the outsiders settle down in a new country, they begin over time to develop affection for and loyalty to it. And as for their children, they have no other home and grow up with the same loyalties and affections as their indigenous counterparts. The way different groups have settled down in America and become Americanised is an obvious example. The same process occurred in Canada and Australia. And in Britain, too, once the Huguenots, the Irish and the Jews settled down, they were soon second to none in their loyalty to the country. Loyalties and affections do not grow in a vacuum. They are a complex product of gratitude, past memories, self-interest and hopes for the future, and have nothing to do with race. If the new groups are shabbily or unfairly treated, they may understandably develop resentment and ill-will. Obviously the host society cannot hound, humiliate or harass them and then expect them to develop affection for it. Affection must obviously be mutual or else it is a form of emotional and moral blackmail.

The attempt to ground the sense of nationality in the unity of stock or kind runs into several other difficulties, and is refuted by Britain's own

40

historical experience. The English do not constitute a homogeneous stock and are a product of a long process of racial intermingling. Yet this has not prevented them from developing a strong sense of nationality. Again the Welsh and the Scots belong, at any rate once did, to a different stock, and had no sense of kinship with the English. Although the memories of war and oppression still rankle and the hostility has not wholly disappeared, they have over the centuries developed a shared sense of loyalty to Britain.

The process of evolution of the British stock did not end with the creation of Great Britain. It went on to absorb such other 'races' as the Huguenots, the Jews and the Irish, all of whom now form part of the British stock. Alfred Sherman and many others like him who evidently feel intensely patriotic towards Britain do not belong to the British stock, and were until a few decades ago immigrants viewed with just the same hostility that they today display towards their black fellow-immigrants. During the colonial period the British rulers married or more often had liaisons with black and brown races, and left behind many a man and woman who can rightly claim, although not prove, a British parent or a grand-parent and may perhaps belong to the British stock. With its entry into the Common Market, Britain has conferred upon the Europeans an unhindered right to settle in Britain and over time become part of the British stock. In short, the British stock has been and is constantly expanding, and its evolutionary process cannot be arbitrarily ended or its boundaries closed at a convenient point in history.

It is not clear upon what evidence the third proposition is based. Over the centuries different immigrant groups have settled in Britain and become integrated into British society. Not one of them has remained an 'alien wedge'. One should have thought that this would be true of the blacks too. The West Indians share with the British their language, religion and a large part of their history. Their only real distinguishing feature is colour, and there is no reason why that should stop them from integrating into British society. Indeed, they came to Britain thinking it to be their mother country and full of loyalty to it. Their colour did not stop them from thinking so, and nor did it stop the British from encouraging them to think so. Their colour acquired importance only later and largely because British society used it to identify and discriminate against them. They did not invent colour-consciousness; rather it was foisted upon them. Furthermore, no evidence is offered of their so-called hatred of Britain. And it is sheer intolerance to suggest that one cannot be said to love Britain if one criticises it, protests against its injustices, retains one's difference or maintains ties with one's country of origin. The charge that the Afro-Caribbeans reject and resent Britain is at best an illicit generalisation from an extremely limited and highly untypical evidence of riots. An overwhelming number of them quietly go about their business.

And one needs to ask if British society itself does not bear a good deal of the responsibility for the hostility of those who do not.

As for the Asians they are said to be profoundly different and 'most unlikely' to identify themselves with Britain. It is difficult to assign clear meaning to such vague and indeterminate assertions. Since the Asians are also said to be intelligent, industrious, peaceable, law-abiding and possessing most of the petty bourgeois virtues, they would seem to be profoundly similar to the British! It is true that some of their customs, religions and cultural practices are different. This was also once true of the Welsh and the Scots, and later, of the Huguenots and the Jews who are all now happily integrated. Even today a relatively small percentage of Jews marry outsiders, and yet no one would accuse them of being an alien wedge. There is no reason why the Asians should be viewed differently. Their differences do not threaten the integrity of the British State which is all that should ultimately matter, and are closely tied up with their virtues.

Besides, customs and practices are never static. As people settle down in a new environment, they undergo a process of cultural adaptation and come closer to the host communities. One really wonders whence the prophets of doom acquire their spurious powers or prescience.

As for the last proposition, we have already said enough to refute it. Modern states are by their very nature composed of different races, religions and cultures, and necessarily multi-national. Nationhood is not at all a practicable ideal for them. Nor is it a desirable ideal, for the glory of the modern State consists in creating a non-natural or non-biological basis of unity and uniting people with nothing in common save the State itself. Further what characterises Britain as a civilised society is its liberal tradition of tolerance and respect for individuals and groups holding different beliefs. The tradition has taken a long time to develop, and is a result of centuries of wars and conflicts. It is suicidal and profoundly illiberal to suggest that Britain should give it up and resort to the crazy and inherently implausible schemes of repatriation and forcible assimilation in order to attain the regressive and inherently impracticable goal of nationhood.

Repatriation and forcible assimilation, further, have very little practical meaning. Over half the black Britons were born in Britain and have no other home. Even after large-scale repatriation of the first-generation blacks, several hundred thousand will still remain. The basic project of keeping Britain white is therefore inherently unrealistic. A move by Britain in this direction cannot but provoke a countermove against it, and there are bound to be trade reprisals and expulsions of Britons settled abroad. Forcible assimilation is just as absurd. Over the years British culture has become considerably diversified and it is not clear what the blacks are to be assimilated into. Further, every culture has a religious basis, and therefore the blacks cannot be fully assimilated unless they were all forcibly converted to Christianity. Again, full assimilation can occur only if begun at birth, and this requires that the blacks should be forced to marry the whites. Once the apparently innocent idea of cultural assimilation is unpacked, one begins to see its mischievous and dangerous implications. One may even wonder if a nation that forcibly broke into other peoples' lands and whose rulers retained a god-like distance from their subjects can talk about repatriation and assimilation without incurring the charges of impertinence, inconsistency and crass hypocrisy. Leaders of public opinion do grave disservice to their country when they take advantage of its legitimate anxieties and understandable confusions to peddle puerile fantasies and seductive but suicidal recipes.

1. Peregrine Worsthorne writes regularly in the *Daily Telegraph* and Roger Scruton in *The Times*. From time to time the two newspapers have also carried articles by Alfred Sherman and Enoch Powell. Scruton's *The Meaning of Conservatism*, Maurice Cowling's *Conservative Essays* and Enoch Powell's collected speeches are also relevant. As for John Casey, I have relied on his 'One Nation : The Politics of Race' in *Salisbury Review, Autumn 1982*. Ian Crowther's *'Mrs. Thatcher's Idea of Good Society'* and Donald Levy's *'On Being Right'* respectively. *The Salisbury Review*, Spring 1983 and Autumn 1982, are also of some interest.
2. *Daily Telegraph* 3 October 1985.

Answers to questions

Q. Gradually, from the 1960s to the present, it has no longer been regarded as deporable to admit that immigration controls are based upon colour. I think it is a new factor but I don't think it is associated specifically with the Right. We find it in the Labour Party and in so called non-political people.

A. It has become quite fashionable to acknowledge being a racist or to say that there is nothing wrong in racism. I believe this happened for the first time in the mid-1970s with an article in the *Daily Telegraph* by Alfred Sherman called 'Racism is not a Sin'. He did not deny that he was a racist but redefined the term so as to mean simply, 'I like to live with people of my own kind'.

On whether New Right ideas are common to the Left as well, one has to be careful with what one means by 'Left' — I was simply thinking of lots of people in the Labour party who would freely accept all the propositions that I have mentioned. Otherwise you cannot explain Merlyn Rees as Home Secretary, following policies which were no different from what David Waddington is following, or the fact that the virginity tests which were first publicised in 1979 had in fact gone on for several years. Certain New Right ideas seem to have infiltrated the Home Office and a large body of opinion on both the Right and the Left.

New Right Theories and the Politicians
William Keegan

William Keegan, of the *Observer,* **describes how New Right theories in economics have influenced particular British politicians and have been translated into policy. The result has been great changes in social and economic structure, with dire effects on the most vulnerable groups in society.**

At a very fundamental level I'm not at all sure that there is a strong or general connection between the New Right theories and the politicians conducting policies. The New Right in politics bases its policies on the old belief in market forces with a few new theories tacked on: they form a small but powerful group. I think what we have seen in this country in the past ten years is a curious mixture of these old and new strands evolving. My jobs over this period at the *Financial Times*, on secondment to the Bank of England, and more recently at the *Observer*, have given me an excellent opportunity to observe and discuss policies with those directly responsible for their making. I've met with not only the opponents and the critics of the New Right, but also with academic monetarists and with many of the people in the Cabinet, both 'wets' and 'drys'. This has sometimes meant meetings with Ministers in obscure Indian curry houses. Of course a rendezvous with a journalist critical of the New Right appears as something else in their engagement diaries.

The main strand of the New Right movement consists of a revival of anti-intervention attitudes and anti-State feeling: less government, in favour of market forces, misconstrued as greater freedom for the individual. I don't think, however that race relations, the main concern of this Trust, ever came into the discussions or thoughts of the New Right explicitly, with the single and well-known exception of Enoch Powell's views of some years ago — which we are told have now changed. It is obvious, however that a government which takes risks with the social structure — which is what I believe them to have done — allows the stone to be lifted and opens the way for old fashioned extreme right wing fascists to get together in the manner, and with the arguments, of such 1930s groups. That there is not a particular attitude towards race is not the same thing as saying that these politicians do not have prejudices. The revival of prejudices against the working class and the poor obviously includes the poor blacks in Britain. So far the damage the New Right have done to the social structure has been manifest in isolated riots. There have been fewer public disturbances than I would have expected. This seems to bear out the prediction made by Professor Galbraith some years ago, which was to the effect that if you were going to conduct a lunatic monetarist experiment what better people to inflict it on than the phlegmatic British who would put up with anything?

With which politicians did the New Right begin? Enoch Powell was the only British politician under the Heath administration to flirt with the New Right and monetarism in some form. He had acolytes: John Biffen, who subsequently became a Cabinet minister, and Terence Higgins were the most notable. Under Heath these people were questioning the Keynesian policies of the time and propounding simple versions of monetarism. The politician who sired Thatcher (if I may use a horse racing term), in an intellectual sense, was Sir Keith Joseph. He did all the serious reading and work on the ideas Thatcher espoused when she came to power in the Tory party in 1975 and subsequently into office in 1979. But there was no generally accepted, well-considered 'New Right' doctrine in the Conservative party in these early days, (nor has there ever been).

Until the late 1970s the New Right in this country, outside a very small band, was not taken seriously within the party they hijacked. Thatcher did not, in my view, rise to office as leader of the Conservative party on the strength of any well-considered doctrine. The move against Heath was personal. Monetarism was not taken seriously and a number of people I have talked to from the Cabinet and among the political advisers were flabbergasted when they realised what had happened. The same goes for the civil servants in Whitehall and my former colleagues at the Bank of England. They couldn't believe who was in charge nor could they believe what determined the policy direction.

As regards theory: Friedman's role is well-recognised. Beyond this, the politicians have adopted the theories of those whose prejudices and, to be generous, sincere beliefs they suit. Their interpretations have not always been accurate. Two names which have been besmirched by the New Right in their quest for support for their beliefs in unhindered market forces are those of Adam Smith and Karl Popper. Adam Smith's writings are full of special cases and the pragmatic necessity for the State to intervene to mitigate the excesses of the invisible hand of the market. He is particularly in favour of government intervention at a local rather than a national level — something that the people who are doing things in his name have very obviously forgotten. The other, Karl Popper, also advocated intervention to assist the economically weak. The stability of institutions is a central issue in his work; this philosopher, so often quoted by Cabinet Ministers flirting with the New Right, asks 'How can we so organise political institutions that bad or incompetent rulers could be prevented from doing too much damage?' The New Right have brought this debate back into the ring.

I would also add that not only do the New Right mis-quote their chosen philosophers, they misrepresent the intellectual opposition's position. This is nowhere more in evidence than in their attitude to the unions. The concern about trade union power is not the prerogative of the New Right. It is an issue which has been concerning, in one form or another, the entire political spectrum. It is not inconsistent to be a Keynesian and to be worried about the apparent strength and occasional irresponsibility of the large unions in the 1970s and 1980s in Britain. The New Right likes to say that the Keynesians love the unions; this is not necessarily true. I think that there is a problem with the structure of the unions in this country, but I would suggest that the correct way to address the problem is to seek improvements in the union structure , not to beat them and abolish them because they cause difficulties.

There is aso an international aspect: the move to the right came simultaneously on both sides of the Atlantic, providing mutual support. There are however, differences. President Reagan was a great deal more pragmatic in the face of recession, and although the Americans continue to call their policies supply-side economics, they indulged in a very obvious Keynesian reflation. This is not to say, of course, that American society represents a desirable alternative; they are stil less inclined to look after their poor than the Europeans.

What has the New Right group of the government done while in power? From 1979 onwards we have had a government with a belief in the free market. The belief in the free market is fair enough; most economists of left, right or centre — Keynesian, monetarist or whatever — believe that the price mechanism is a better mechanism than centralised decision making in many aspects of the economy. But the New Right believe that the market should operate everywhere. The cutting of public sector borrowing has become an obsession (I should like to point out that under the Heath administration of 1970-74 Joseph and Thatcher were the biggest spenders of public money) based on Thatcher's belief that the nation should run the way a household is presumed to run: with balanced books. Not only did this fly in the face of Keynesian belief that it was the government's role to borrow in order to make use of unemployed resources to produce real goods, it also does not stand up when measured against a typical household which borrows beyond its current means quite a lot of the time.

The belief in the free market extended to the view that the exchange rate should be determined by market forces. The New Right also adopted Professor Friedman's notion that they could control inflation by controlling the money supply — only someone forgot to ask what the money supply was and whether we could control it even if we knew.

The consequence of this was an extraordinary period in 1979-81 when wage inflation reached 28%, the retail price index was rising at a rate of 22% per annum and the exchange rate was allowed to rise from $1.70 to $2.45. To cut a long story short, the result was that British industry was being priced out of world markets. There is an anecdote which captures the essence of all this: in the autumn of 1980 the Chairman of ICI went to Number 10 Downing Street and asked Thatcher if it was her wish for ICI to stay in business. ICI was being squeezed by the general explosion in costs consequent on Thatcher's policy; ICI needed her to do something about it. Thereafter the 'hands-off-everything-except-public-sector-borrowing' approach became just a little more pragmatic. There was a certain amount of intervention in the exchange markets and the exchange rate did fall.

Other problems, however became more evident to the public at large than ICI's profit performance. Wage inflation and price inflation are now down to around 9% and 7% respectively, but unemployment is, according to the government's figures 3.3m, according to most others, 4m. The unemployment figures are the testimony to the extent of the recession. All this stuff about recovery has to be taken with a heavy dose of salt. The years 1979 to 1982 saw the most severe recession since the war — real GDP fell by 4% and the subsequent growth has taken us back to a little above (6%) where we were in 1979; nearly half of this growth was accounted for by North Sea oil production. And still most economic forecasters are not predicting a fall in unemployment.

The contribution made by North Sea oil is worth looking at in more detail. Although the oil will not run out until the year 2000 or beyond, the dynamic contribution from the North Sea is over and the only question is at what rate revenues fall and the helpful contribution to the balance of payments lessens. They of the New Right had no policy on oil, and now it is too late to turn the tide. Thanks to North Sea oil, during the period 1980-82 Britain ran the biggest balance of payments surplus of any industrialised country; for once the familiar arguments about growth being constrained by balance of payments consideration waned, but, so now has the balance of payments surplus. During this time of unprecedented opportunity about one-fifth of the manufacturing capacity of this country disappeared. The expansion that hasn't yet happened may now run into a balance of payments constraint. It is the most extraordinary waste of a national resource. A testimony to the absence of policy and trust in the market.

That is the past. How has this experience impacted on the New Right? Power rests very much in the hands of Thatcher and Lawson, but there has been something of a Cabinet revolt. Biffen, an early convert to monetarism, has begun to worry that the level of public spending is too low; he seems to have joined Peter Walker and the other wets. Peter Walker is, however, the only wet left in the Cabinet; the others have been fired. The opinion polls would suggest that the support for the economic policies pursued by Thatcher is weakening; there is the beginnings of a political trend moving against Thatcher and the Chancellor. I suspect, however, that Thatcher would sack her Chancellor if her position was perceived to be seriously threatened by the economic policies of the New Right. There is certainly some chance of that. Whichever way you look at it, the inflation problem in this country has not been solved despite the heavy costs imposed on our resources both human and natural. Galbraith was right, we have tolerated the kind of hardship that we would never have expected to see again. But how far can this go? I don't know. Indeed in the wake of the riots contributed to, in my opinion, by the New Right's attrition of the social structure, the law and order ticket may seem to offer Thatcher some breathing space.

I would like to conclude by admitting that I am a two-handed economist: I am both an optimist and a pessimist. I am optimistic because I think the economic policies of. this government have been shown for what they are, that this is being more widely recognised and that the heyday is over. I am pessimistic because I think the damage that has been done is immense; we do need to reconstruct the economy and rescue the social structure. It is a post war position in many ways and while solutions are not intellectually difficult to envisage a political consensus does seem elusive at least in the foreseeable future.

Answers to questions

Q. Do you see any particular connection between the way in which the economy is likely to develop and the exacerbation or alleviation of racial tensions in this country?

A. I think that the consensus now developing in the country from the opinion polls and what the Conservative politicians always call the message from the doorsteps, is that this level of unemployment is intolerable and something has got to be done. If that is the message, and people are wanting to act on it, that must be good for race relations. A preponderance of people also now say they think the public spending cuts have gone too far. Public spending cuts hit the poor and deprived of all colours. A change here would bring new hope.

Q. The experience in Australia and New Zealand has been that the rhetoric of the New Right has so influenced the political agenda that the

incoming Labour governments in both countries have actually retained, in economic policies anyway, the same rhetoric and have put New Right policies into practice. So what happens in this country if that influence is retained here? Suppose a Labour government does come in, but is still influenced to win the middle ground sufficiently to retain some of those policies?

A. Fair point. I think the same has happened to a certain extent in French economic policy. The left wing of the Tory party and the Social Democrats and the Liberals, despite some lip service paid by David Owen to economic policies which might be described as New Right are crystal clear on Keynesian versus Monetarist policies. I think they also have clear ideas about where the bias should be in distribution policies of taxation and public expenditure. I don't think that the New Right has forever moved them away from areas that they will never return to. But I think it has put a tremendous onus on them to avoid giving hostages to fortune by making foolish promises of the kind that the Labour party made in 1974-75 in this country.

There is a new, I think encouraging and healthy, more outward-looking movement, call it European if you like, within the British Left. There are very few people there now who think that 'Fortress Britain' is the answer in economic policy, that you can just put up the shutters on Britain. They are talking more in a European context about protectionist policies, if they believe in protectionist policies.

Secondly, when it comes to expansionary and Keynesian policies they are now thinking more in European terms. The OECD has done some extremely good work on all this, on concerted expansion. There is a much wider awareness that Europe should be getting its act together and there should be more concerted economic policy in Europe.

The New Right in France and the Federal Republic of Germany

Franz Gress

Franz Gress, Professor of Social Science at Frankfurt University, describes the New Right in France and Germany, and how the intellectual movements there, unlike the New Right in Britain and the United States, are strongly opposed to a conservative establishment. Nationalistic and antiegalitarian, they are also radical, and adopt the kind of style and appeal we would associate here more with the Left.

I would like to give you some preliminary results based on a research project which started in 1982, and should be concluded at the end of 1986. The subject is the 'New Right' in the Federal Republic of Germany, France and Great Britain.

The method is a primarily descriptive and inductive one, as we think in such a field of research which is so highly affected by moral and political judgement, it is of no use at all to work with catchwords like 'fascists', 'neo-nazis' etc. We accepted the term 'New Right' which was coined for the French GRECE (Group for Research and Study on European Civilisation/Groupement de Récherche et d'Études pour la Civilisation Européene) and later was accepted by them. The analytical dimensions has to be kept separated as much and as long as possible from the value-dimension which should be brought in at the last phase of the project, evaluating the results.

Looking at the sources, especially printed materials and interviews, one can sum up: the New Right is not a centralised organisation or conspiracy, it is a form of *ideological action*, which sees itself as a challenge and response to the spiritual poverty of western societies. It is a sort of European *intellectual network*, where people know each other — often more than their writings reveal — and influencing each other to and fro, and it is obviously inspired by the ideas and partial success of GRECE. Its members are in a certain way intellectuals. They do not display *Mein Kampf*. They are often more Bohemian or academic in lifestyle than traditional conservatives, whom they do not want to resemble at all.

I think that there is a genuine strand in the Right today which is neither neo-nazi nor conservative in argumentation. In particular, persons and

51

publications of this ideological brand do not mention, or link themselves to, the interwar *systems* of Fascism or Nazism. Thus they are distinct from the traditional far Right, whose intellectual wing for some years has been occupied with white-washing the Third Reich by denying the fact of the Holocaust (e.g. Rassinier Stäglich, Christopherson, Butz and last but not least, in a very special way, David Irving).

By contrast, the New Right does not see itself as conservative in any way. Armin Mohler, the leading figure of the German Right speaks willingly of himself as a right-winger, regarding present day conservatism as merely a mongrel liberal-conservatism.

And I think P Vial, one of the founders and leading members of GRÉCE, aimed in the same direction when he told the audience at the 'Colloque National' in November 1984:

> Je me moquais, il y a vingt ans de mes copains étudiants qui punaisaient dans leur chambres le portrait du Che Guevara. J'avais tort. Che Guevara représentait symboliquement pour eux, et il représente aujourd'hui pour moi, la seule espérance qui vaille. Celle de se battre pour essayer de changer un monde insupportable. Le monde de la petite jouissance médiocre, de la combine et de la loi du tric.[1]

From this it is obvious, that the term New Right in Europe refers to a group which is different from what is called New Right in the USA. There, New Right means the gospel that 'man is born Friedman but everywhere he is in Keynes'. The New Right in Europe, on the contrary, is the absolute enemy of *laissez-faire* capitalism and the state of society it produces. Or as the leading theorist of GRECE Alain de Benoist says in looking at the USA and the USSR, 'Decay is worse than dictatorship'.

Common ideas of the New Right in Eurpe are: Antiegalitaranism; philosophically, they are nominalist. From this follows the rejection of general historical laws on the other (Liberalism and Marxism).

But nevertheless they are not individualistic: 'Individualism is the common denominator of liberalism and Marxism', says A de Benoist who believes it was created by Christian destruction of the original holistic civilisation of Europe.

Though this anti-Christianism is a very special position of Benoist, who has written recently a scholarly book with the title, *How to be a Pagan*, this example demonstrates how far removed is the New Right in Europe from conservatism and the old Right. A look into the *Salisbury Review* shows you how much this organ of right-wing Tory ideology is connected with a conservative tradition of Christianity as in the mainstream of British culture. On the other hand it is not by chance that J. Evola, the fascist-paganist author is often quoted, as well as Nietzsche, by the

European New Right. The only English journal representing this strand of the New Right advertised: 'Read the Scorpion ... The only Nietzschean inspired cultural review in Britain' (*Spectator* 16.7.83).

Ethnopluralism (in the sense of resistance to imperialism and internationalism) is the positive expression for the New Right of their antiegalitarianism. One of the last national meetings of GRECE was devoted to 'Le cause des peuples', stressing the right to cultural identity of the peoples of Europe and the Third World against US-capitalist economic exploitation and cultural dominance. In Germany all three main papers of the New Right refer to this ethnopluralistic position by subtitles.

"Neue Zeit" — Forum für die sache der Völker
"Wir Selbst" (by the way the translation of Sinn Fein) — Zeitschrift für nationale Identität und internationale Solidarität)
"Aufbruch" Beiträge zur nationalrevolutionären Politik

Unlike the traditional right, the New Right does not argue in sociobiological terms, or at least does not put these arguments in the front line. Only up to 3% of the longer articles in the French GRECE quarterly *Éléments* (subtitle: La Revue de la Nouvelle Droite) deal with biology, sociobiology or ethnology, but a third of all longer articles refer to *cultural* identity or deal with the question of nationhood and cultures. The other magazine of the French New Right, *Nouvelle Ecole* contained, up to 1979, about 13% of texts which dealt with biology. Here again there is a contrast with conservative positions like those of R Scruton with his concept of the Hegelian/Schmitt authoritarian state. But views on these issues vary within the camp of the New Right. Not everybody likes the concept of 'Balkanisation for everybody', which was developed by one of its former sympathisers.

International politics, according to this concept, is centred around the idea of self-determination of a people. On the one hand, the nationalist revolutionary forces approve of the independent development of Third World countries *(auto-zentrierte entwicklung)*, with strong sympathies for national liberation movement such as the PLO, IRA, Greenland before it left the EEC (Aufbruch) and Colonel Gaddafi's experiment (Wir Selbst). On the other hand the New Right, especially in the case of GRECE, thinks the western alignment must be got rid of. Europe is under a state of double occupation, and the aim of European politics must be 'to form of Europe an independent, self-sustaining, self-sufficient power' (A de Benoist). A leading figure of British neo-conservatism thinks this is mere wishful thinking and reveals utter ignorance of the USSR. But nevertheless, A de Benoist would prefer to wear the cap of the Red Army than to live in Brooklyn for the rest of his days on hamburgers.

Some concluding remarks in a theoretical and political direction: Since the sixties the Right in France and the Federal Republic of Germany has tried to get rid of the stigma of the Nazi era. It has become obvious that the traditional way of attaining political power through electoral politics is not (except sometimes in the short term) successful for the Right. Electoral strategies are still followed by the older generation of the Right but a small group has broken away and formed a New Right by trying to collect together the remnants of the "Konservative Revolution", reflecting those anti-western and anti-liberal traditions of thinking from Nietzsche onwards which were forerunners as well as victims of Nazism. The New Right goes close to the brink of fascism itself — fascism as distinct from Nazism — when it refers to national socialism and to authors like J Evola. Meanwhile the New Right everywhere uses new forms of political communication and access to the public. It is not afraid to reach out towards and even adopt the Left in what it calls a 'Gramcisme de droite'.

What are the chances of success for this strategy of working outside the institutionalised political process? There are many people who find it attractive to be caught up in new, or apparently new, philosophical and ideological movements which challenge existing, accepted positions. There is a spice of excitement in feeling that one is in fundamental opposition to the traditions of the enlightenment, and that those traditions are crumbling. The argumentative style of the New Right is competely different from the old style of jackboot nationalism and so it can rely on the liberal tradition of free speech. Therefore, simple repression by the authorities is neither possible nor desirable. The only way to curb the spreading of those ideas is the use of the liberal tradition: of discussion, analysis and criticism. We have to argue from historical experience and point out the possible consequences which are connected with such a political philosophy.

1. Twenty years ago I laughed at my fellow students who used to pin up Che Guevara's photograph in their rooms. I was wrong. Che Guevara symbolically represented for them and represents today for me, the only worthwhile hope. The only chance of fighting to attempt to change an intolerable world. I mean a world of petty mediocre pleasures, of old-boy networks and fixers, of fiddling and money grabbing.

Answers to questions

Q. Can you clarify how you would draw a line between the New Right and neo-conservatism?

A. Neo-conservatism has an American branch, which stems mainly from ex-liberals — people like Moynihan and others who were very much engaged in following up the New Deal and the welfare state in the US but then became disappointed by the unintended consequences of those schemes. They reacted by becoming conservative in a very libertarian, thoroughly American, tradition. On the other hand, neo-conservatives in Europe do not come from a liberal background. Their background is the student rebellion of the period between 1965 and 1968. Although the student revolution did not occur in England in the same way that it did on the Continent, it made a great impression on certain people in the younger generation who have now become leaders of the New Right in Great Britain. Their reaction was a desire to convey how impressive, how stimulating, it was to see people going up against the establishment and having ideas. They set up study groups, and these have been used to try to give the Conservative party exciting new ideas. Though they disagreed with the Left, the *method* of ideological development and theoreticisation was very impressive to them. On the Continent, this new theoretical strand in right-wing thinking has grown in a rather different direction. For example, recently the New Right in Germany have expressed sympathy with revolutionary nationalist groups in certain Third World countries, on the ground that colonialism is bad. All peoples have the right to their own identity and cultural surroundings, and their own territory: so nationalism is the justification for such anti-colonial revolutionary groups.

At the same time, the New Right and the neo-conservatives in Germany are both traditional in the sense that, like such people in Britain, they want their own society to be a society of people of the same stock.

The Runnymede Trust

The Runnymede Trust is a registered educational charity set up in 1968. Its objectives are the collection and dissemination of information and the promotion of public education on immigration and race relations. This is done in a number of ways:

- An information service which provides information on race and immigration.
- A reference library of books, pamphlets and press cuttings which may be used by prior appointment.
- A monthly bulletin, *Race and Immigration*.
- Publication of pamphlets and papers on matters of current interest and concern.
- Seminars and meetings.

A full list of publications and details of subscriptions to *Race and Immigration* are available on request.

Runnymede Trust
178 North Gower Street
London NW1 2NB
01-387 8943